HIGHLIGHTS OF THE HIGHLANDS CENTER

AND

LYNX LAKE AREA OF ARIZONA

A NATURALIST'S VIEW

PHOTOGRAPHY AND TEXT BY

AL LODWICK

VOLUNTEER NATURALIST

HIGHLANDS CENTER FOR NATURAL HISTORY

PRESCOTT, ARIZONA

First Edition 2014

Second Edition 2015

ISBN 978-0-9897751-1-3

Dedication

To Ann Lodwick whose love and shared interests have supported me for nearly thirty-eight years.

Foreword

The mission of the Highlands Center for Natural History is to help children and adults to discover the wonders of nature and become wise caretakers of the land.

In 2011 Al Lodwick enrolled in the naturalist program to receive the advanced training we require of people who are going to lead unscripted nature walks on the center's Lynx Creek site and other venues around Prescott. Since graduating from the training he has led dozens of walks for hundreds of people exploring the natural beauty of the area.

Al is rarely seen without a camera around his neck and even when this occurs he has one stashed in a pocket somewhere. Many of his pictures have been used in our publications and in various slide shows.

The Highlands Center has free trail guides available to give basic details about our area. This book is designed to be a supplement to add to your enjoyment. Al has agreed to donate a portion of the profits from the sale of this book to further the mission of the Highlands Center for Natural History.

Dave Irvine, Executive Director
Highlands Center for Natural History
April 2014

Introduction

For almost five years I have lived in and photographed the area within three miles of the Highlands Center for Natural History and Lynx Lake. During this time there have been only a few days that I did not take pictures of at least birds in my yard. Admittedly, the pictures are not all of the quality that you would find in national publications. They were all taken with relatively inexpensive cameras. There were no attempts to attract the subjects, except for some bird feeders in my yard and no elaborate set-ups were used; not even a tripod. They represent what any person walking through the area is likely to encounter at the appropriate time of the year, except for a few of the pictures were taken under controlled conditions.

The Highlands Center for Natural History offers many classes each year in fulfilling its mission of helping children and adults discover the wonders of nature and become wise caretakers of the land. Taking many of these classes has led to my certification as a Naturalist.

I have also volunteered for the Prescott National Forest, helping people to appreciate what they are seeing as they enjoy being in nature.

Some new ideas for things to do on the trails are offered such as looking for faces in the gnarly Arizona White Oaks.

My hope is that this book will stimulate your curiosity and encourage you to add new perspectives in your encounters with nature. I am convinced that spending so much time in natural surroundings has prolonged my life.

Al Lodwick

Prescott, Arizona

July 2015

Acknowledgements

Sue Arnold for technical assistance.

Brandi Lee Cooper for help with identifications and insights into habitats.

Jill Craig for guiding my projects in the naturalist program.

Charlie De Marco, M.S. for technical assistance.

Bob Gessner for technical assistance with the "Lichens and Fungi" section.

Maurine Haeberlin for the original idea of the book.

Tony Krzysik, Ph.D., Ecologist and Statistician for assistance in preparing the "Reptiles and Amphibian" section.

Ann Lodwick for her ideas and editorial assistance.

Larry Lodwick for species identification.

Rachel Lodwick for the Mieswick, LLC logo.

Scott Mies for inspiration and technical assistance.

Fiona Reid for founding the naturalist program at the Highlands Center for Natural History and accepting me into the program.

Sue Smith, President, Prescott Chapter – Arizona Native Plant Society for plant identification.

Victoria Tubbs for the author's photo.

BIRDS

Bald Eagle

The Bald Eagle is at the top of the pecking order. It rarely gives way to any other bird. The most likely place to see one is in the dead trees (called snags) on the east side of Lynx Lake. Look for it outlined against the sky as it sits and looks for its favorite food, fish. At the Highlands Center it is most often seen in flight. There is a nesting pair in the area during most years. Occasionally they can be seen together. Both males and females develop the white (bald) head but only when they are at least four years old. They perch in a mostly vertical position and have prominent shoulders. Typically the adult birds are about 36 inches in length. The females are slightly larger. If you are looking for one across the lake remember that you are looking for something the size of a yardstick about the length of four football fields away. They will not look huge at this distance.

When diving for prey, these birds can reach speeds of 100 miles per hour. They weigh about 10 pounds. Their talons can grip with a force of 400 pounds per square inch. For reference, a human grip is about 40 pounds per square inch. Imagine being hit with something that weighs 10 pounds moving at 100 miles per hour and being squeezed 10 times harder than a human can. Most prey is killed almost instantaneously.

They seem to have increased in number to the point that I have seen them in the area during every month of the year. Some of them may be only migrating,

Great Blue Heron

The largest heron in North America standing four feet tall and with a wingspan of seven feet, this bird goes almost anywhere it wants. Where it wants to go is next to water or where it has a clear view of water. At the Highlands Center it is most often seeing flying overhead with its slow, powerful wing beats. In flight, its legs are held out behind the tail. It usually hunts by standing motionless in the water waiting for prey to come into range. It then strikes with a swift thrust, often pushing its sharp, heavy beak completely through a fish.   It is often mistaken for a crane but cranes are very unusual in this habitat. When Lynx Lake hasn't been stocked with fish for a while, they will attempt to take a fish caught by other birds and even people.

Common Raven

Ravens are sometimes mistaken for crows. However, crows are very unusual in this habitat. Ravens make all sorts of noises from pairs making soft, cooing noises (heard around this area in late winter) to harsh noises that sound like adolescents arguing (in the summer). These vocalizations can go on for extended periods of time.

Ravens will eat anything that is available. Driving down Walker Road you will sometimes see them feasting on road-kill. You think that they will not fly and you are sure that you will hit one. However, they usually manage to get away.

During nesting season you may see them chasing a bald eagle that has gotten too close to their nest. In turn, you will often see them being chased by much smaller birds that are defending their nests. Ravens share the top of the pecking order with eagles and great blue herons. They are not afraid of the larger birds but neither are they very successful in competitions against them. In the top left picture you will see a raven using weapons (chunks of wood) dropping them on a bald eagle in an attempt to get the eagle to leave after it landed below where the raven was already perched. Flying straight at you, a raven looks very much like a stealth fighter.

Osprey

Ospreys have a troubled past at Lynx Lake. They were the top of the fish-eating food chain for many years. When the pesticide DDT was banned one of the main beneficiaries was the bald eagle. As the bald eagle population grew they needed to take over osprey habitat to keep expanding. One of the places they took over was Lynx Lake. In every interaction between these two species that I have witnessed the bald eagle has been dominant. I have twice witnessed an osprey catch a fish and a bald eagle immediately attack the osprey and cause it to drop its catch. After one incident someone commented that it was the third time that they had witnessed it that morning. Twice I watched an osprey try to force a bald eagle to leave its spot in a tree but the eagle refused to move. Who would have guessed that banning DDT would have had such a deleterious effect on osprey? However, they are better off than in the 1960s when Arizona Game Wardens were instructed to shoot them on sight because they ate so many fish that were stocked in the lakes for people to catch.

Osprey hunt in a unique manner, flying slowly, even hovering, over water until they spot a likely prey, then they tuck their head between their feet and go into a high speed dive into the water with both feet and the head hitting the water simultaneously. They submerge, chasing the fish.

Mallard

This duck loves to be around people.   Mallards have been domesticated for centuries. I have witnessed a mother lead her brood of very small babies up onto the shore and right through a seated human family with small children. If you are walking along the shore of Lynx Lake and hear, "Quack, Quack, Quack," it almost a sure thing that you are hearing a mallard's call.

The main source of food for mallards is vegetation that grows in shallow water. They harvest these by putting their head down in to the water and pointing their tail skyward. However, most wild creatures are opportunists that will not turn away from any easy source of nutrition. Mallards have been observed eating the carcasses of dead fish.

Mallards nest along the shore concealed by the vegetation there. This is a big reason to not let dogs run loose around the lake. Dogs can destroy the nest and female mallards can be quite aggressive when protecting their nests.

During the breeding season (late winter and spring) the male has a bright green head. (In some light conditions it can appear bluish.) In the summer the male's feathers turn brown and it becomes difficult to tell the sexes apart. The male's green head reappears in the fall.

Double-Crested Cormorant

This bird is named for the feathery patches that it develops in breeding season that look like hairy ears. Cormorants go after fish by floating on the surface of the lake and then submerging to swim underwater to catch their prey. They swallow smaller fish while underwater but often bring larger prey to the surface to swallow it. An osprey will attack a cormorant with a fish hanging from its mouth. I witnessed a cormorant with a snake hanging from both sides of its beak like a Fu-Manchu mustache. After some gyrations the snake was swallowed whole just before an osprey arrived to do battle. Unlike most birds living largely on the water they do not have oil glands that keep their feathers waterproof. Consequently they seem to ride very low in the water. They frequently go to a dead tree and sun themselves while extending their wings to dry their feathers. If you hear about ten rapid splashes in the water and quickly locate the source you will be able to see a cormorant running on the surface of the water while flapping its wings in its extended take-off maneuver.

Cooper's Hawk

This is the most common hawk in the area. It nests in some of the taller Ponderosa Pine trees on the Highlands Center property. If you are walking on the Stretch Pebble trail around the first of July you will often hear this bird making loud, threatening noises from a tree perch. My wife experienced being brushed on the back of her baseball cap while walking away from an aggressive Cooper's hawk. It was probably defending a nest.

Birds that prey on other birds are called accipiters. Cooper's hawks are in this category. They will catch other birds while in flight. However, if they know that their prey is hiding in a brushy area they will run around trying to flush out their next meal.

Cooper's Hawks grow very accustomed to being around humans. They will sit for prolonged periods in full view of people. If you see feathers drifting down near tall trees, look up, you may be able to spot a Cooper's hawk enjoying its catch.

In the lower picture on the right notice the rear-facing, almost tooth-like structures in the mouth that will assist in holding captured prey.

The photo on the cover is a Cooper's hawk sitting on a branch in a monsoon rain.

Anna's Hummingbird

If you see a hummingbird in this area there is a good chance that it is an Anna's. These are the first hummers show-up each year. They usually appear even before the last snowfall of the season. Some people claim that this is because feeders have been left out all winter. However, as far back as the 1940s there was speculation among ornithologists that Anna's were somehow able to survive in the mountains through the winter. They may have wintered in the area all along but there were far fewer people in the area to notice them

Anna's are very intelligent birds and accustomed to being around humans. The first February that I lived in the area, I was sitting outdoors when a male flew up and buzzed back and forth right in front of my eyes. He seemed to be telling me that it was my duty to put the feeder out. On some other occasions when the feeder ran low a male would fly up to the window and gently tap once to call our attention to the situation. One morning I was leaning on my walking stick watching a female Anna's around the boat rental area at Lynx Lake. She seemed to be gathering silk from spider webs for her nest. Suddenly she turned and flew right in front of my face and examined my beard. She rejected those coarse hairs but flew over and plucked a hair from my ring finger and made a hasty retreat.

Acorn Woodpecker

Among the land-based birds, this is one of the most commonly seen year-round residents of the area. As the name implies their main source of food through the winter is the acorn. They are stored by the thousands in the trunks of dead ponderosa pines and to a lesser extent in the bark of live trees. This makes it easy for just one or two birds to guard the granary against predation. One curious thing about their habits is that they do not pursue an acorn if it is dropped on the ground. Should it not be discovered by any other creature it can sprout and start a new oak tree.

In the upper left picture note that the bird is not attached to the tree. To take off from the tree trunk they simply tuck their feet and flap their wings.

Males and females are distinguished by the pattern of the cap on the forehead. The pictures in the upper right and lower left are males – the red cap touches the white forehead. Females have a band of black between the red and the white as seen in the picture on the center left.

The eyes of the Acorn Woodpecker favor looking skyward. This makes sense since one of their main dangers comes from Cooper's Hawks overhead. During the summer when last year's acorns have been consumed and the new growth has not matured acorn woodpeckers will eat insects. Since they do not see straight down very well they have developed the ability to rotate their head nearly 180°. This is what the bird in the lower left picture is doing. It is looking for insects in the cracks in the log.

In the upper right picture you can see a male emerging from the nest and also note the holes which can be used to store acorns.

Western Tanager

One would think with all of these bright colors that this bird would be quite easy to spot in a ponderosa pine forest. However, this is not true. Somehow these colors function as camouflage. It can be quite tolerant of humans but it never stays in one place for very long.

White-breasted Nuthatch

White-breasted nuthatches are as comfortable upside down on a tree as they are right side up. It can run head first down a tree trunk. It does this when foraging for insects. Seeds are a major part of its diet. When it has a seed that is difficult to crack open it will wedge it into a crevice and hammer on it with its bill until it "hatches".

FLOWERS

Sweet Four O'clock

These flowers are found it late afternoon along Trail 441 on the Highlands Center property in late summer to early fall. This family gets its name from the fact that the flowers bloom late in the afternoon and will disappear by the next morning.

Western Dayflower or Bird-bill Dayflower

It will be hard to see both flowers on this page in the same day even though they bloom in the same seasons and in the same area. This is because the western dayflower blooms about dawn and the flower wilts away by about noon.

Mountain Mahogany

The hairy, spiral parts are actually seed pods and not flowers. When these seed pods drop off the plant they often stick into the ground in a vertical position. When they get wet they straighten out. When they dry out they become curled again. By repeating the process several times over the winter they can actually screw themselves into the ground. This gives the seeds a good chance at germination. Pour a little water on them and watch the process. Look for these in late summer and early autumn

Desert Calico

This plant is part of the phlox family. Look for it in dry, rocky soil. In this area the blooms usually peak in April. It only grows to be about 1 or 2 inches tall. It forms a mat that is almost always less than 12 inches wide. The flowers are symmetrical – if you drew a line down the middle, one side would look like the mirror image of the other.

The flowers may vary in color from white to pink to lavender.

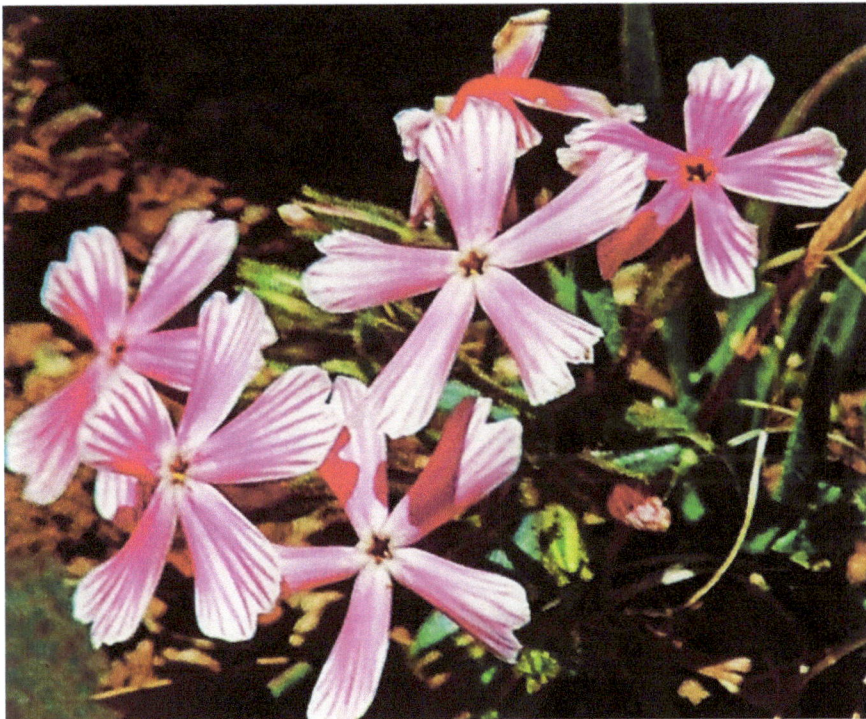

Rattlesnake Weed

Folk medicine declared that this was an effective treatment for rattlesnake bites. However, it is no longer recognized as such by most authorities. In fact, like many members of the spurge family it may be dangerously poisonous itself. That could account for its lack of use today.

You could easily walk past this plant and not notice it because it only grows about half an inch high. Its flowers are tiny also. Look for it at the Lynx Lake North Shore Park around the lookout area during the month of May.

Colorado Four O'clock

Look for this plant in areas where you see alligator juniper trees. It prefers to grow in the shade of larger shrubs. As the name implies, it blooms late in the afternoon and the flowers wilt away in the next morning's sun. It blooms throughout almost all of the warm months.

It is used in traditional medicine. The root is dried and ground into a powder and then moistened and used to cover sore joints. In times of famine it was used to suppress the appetite. It has a side effect that limits its popularity – severe, watery diarrhea.

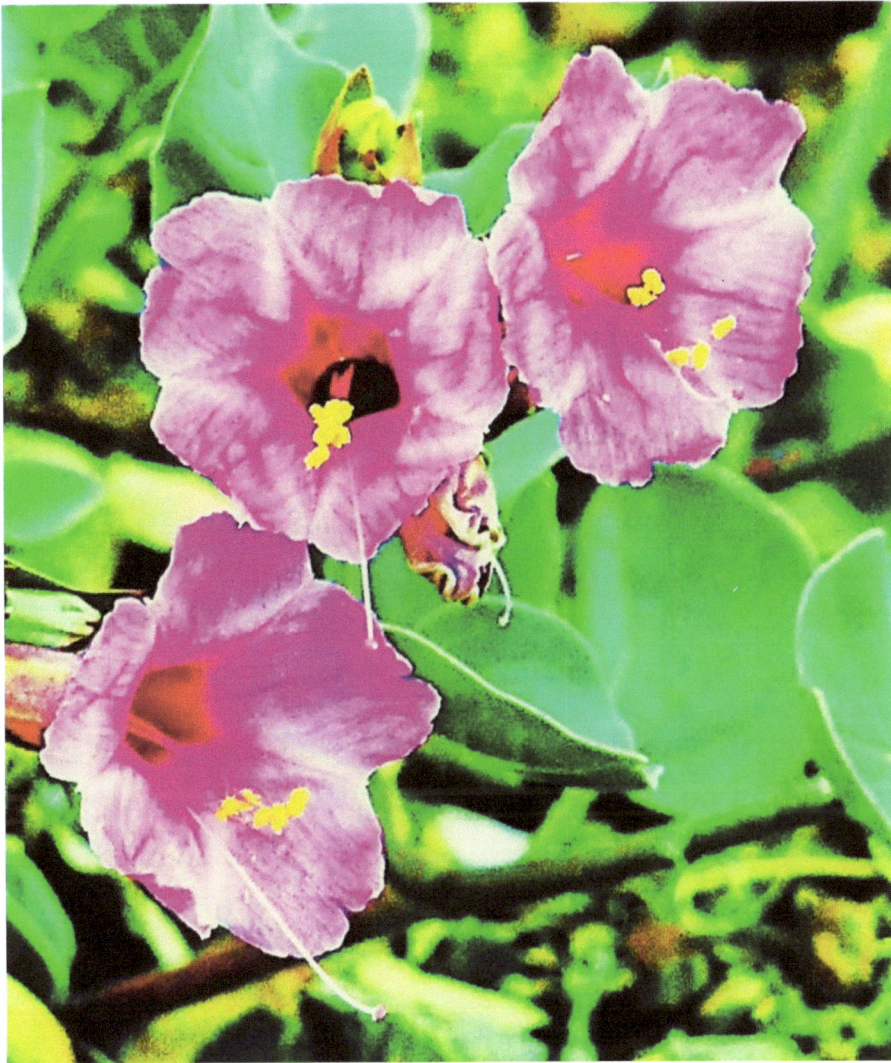

Indian Paintbrush

The paintbrush family has many similar members making it very difficult to distinguish the exact species. One interesting fact is that the red parts are not the flowers. They are bracts – specialized leaves.

These plants concentrate the element selenium from the soils in which they grow. The flowers have been eaten by some native tribes but before you do so remember that the red bracts are not the flowers and selenium overdose can cause hair and fingernail loss.

Scarlet Gilia or Skyrocket

In this area, this will be the most common red flower that you see. It is especially plentiful during July and August. If you are thinking about planting a garden of native plants, this readily grows from seeds. It is also a great hummingbird attracter.

The explorers Lewis and Clark named this plant in 1806 while exploring what is now the northwestern part of the United States.

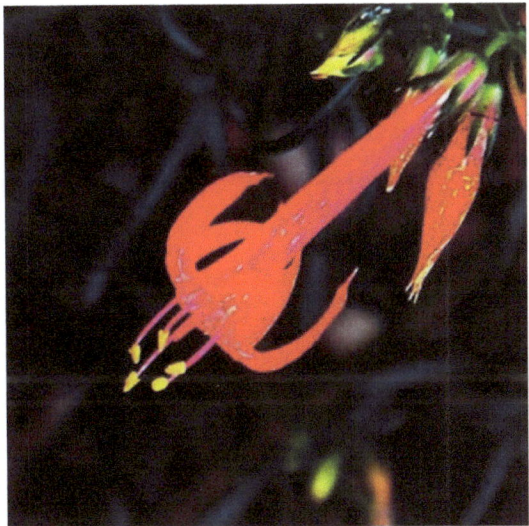

Globemallow

There are both mountain and desert globe mallow growing in this area. They are difficult to tell apart so this will just be called globemallow. It is very common during the summer months. The color of the flowers varies with the soil conditions in which it is growing. It can be very difficult for digital cameras to record the color accurately and printing the pictures can make the colors even worse. Therefore, do not be concerned if the picture color doesn't exactly match what you are seeing.

Tansy Aster

This plant is often seeded to assist in restoring disturbed areas. It competes well with less desirable species such as cheat grass and knapweed. It is extremely drought tolerant. It grows from one to three feet tall, so it is easy to spot.

It has been used by various Native American tribes as a stimulant, for respiratory and gastrointestinal problems.

White Sweet Clover

This is an invasive plant that was brought to the United States about 100 years ago from Germany. It will grow in almost any kind of soil. The hope was that it would serve as a substitute cattle feed for its near relative alfalfa that requires higher quality soil to thrive. Although it thrives in poor soil it did not prove to be as nutritious for cattle as had been hoped. Look for it around the north shore of Lynx Lake in July and August.

These and the yellow plant pictured on the next page are now classified as variations of the same species. There is no significance to the angle that they flowers are pictured.

Yellow Sweet Clover

The sweet clovers were instrumental in developing the drug warfarin (Coumadin®). About 100 years ago when they were imported to the U.S. they were fed to cattle in place of alfalfa. Under certain conditions they fermented a chemical that slowed the cow's ability to form blood clots. As a result cattle died of internal bleeding. In the pre-computer days analyzing data was tediously slow so it took about twenty years to figure out what was happening. Chemists tinkered with the molecule for about another ten years until they figured out that it could be used to kill rats. About fifteen more years of research produced warfarin which is used to prevent or treat blood clots in people still today.

Apache Plume

Apache plume blooms during all of the warm months. Once the seed pods start to form, the shrub will be covered with both blossoms (left picture) and seed pods (right picture). It especially blooms about two weeks after a good monsoon rain. Overall, it likes dry conditions and does not do well after wet winters.

In the local Native American culture a tea made from Apache plume roots was used to make the hair shiny.

Slimleaf Plains Mustard

These flowers are found somewhere in the area in almost any season except winter. The plant grows up to four feet tall but the flowers are only about an inch long, so they are not easy to find. A US Department of Agriculture online map does not show them growing in Yavapai County but I took this picture in the area.

This picture was taken in the early morning after an overnight rain.

Prairie Coneflower

This plant stands from one to four feet high and is common along roadsides. The flowers are at the top of long, leafless stalks. The flowers are from one to three inches long.

There have been many medicinal uses for these plants reported but the conditions for which they have been used could be quite serious, so I would recommend leaving their use to the experienced practitioner.

Salsify

The seeds of this plant resemble a gigantic dandelion. However, this plant is in the sunflower family. Their Latin name is derived from a word that translates to "goat's beard". In the Mediterranean area there is evidence that salsify has been cultivated as a food crop for over 2,000 years. The root has been described as tasting like either an oyster or an artichoke.

Salsify prefers soils that have been disturbed. Since this area was heavily cut for timber, mined for gold, farmed, roads paved, trails laid out and a dam built you might find it almost anywhere during the warm seasons.

Wheeler's Thistle

Butterflies love these flowers. When the butterfly rubs against the male part of the flower it picks up pollen which can then be deposited on the female parts. This causes the seeds to form. When the seeds are mature they develop little "parachutes" and look like miniature versions of the salsify pictured on the previous page. Birds called goldfinches are particularly attracted to these seeds. Look for these flowers from early spring to late summer.

Arizona Thistle

This plant prefers to grow around the edges of ponderosa pine forests. It blooms from late spring to fall. Some guidebooks say that it grows up to four feet tall but I have never seen one more than about two feet tall in this area. Anna's hummingbirds especially favor this plant. For another picture of the Arizona Thistle see page about ants in the insect section.

TREES

Ponderosa Pine

An interesting fact about this tree is that it is NOT the Arizona Ponderosa Pine. This is simply called the Ponderosa Pine. The trees in this area have their needles in groups of three. The Arizona Ponderosa Pine has its needles in groups of five. Another interesting fact is that this area is in the midst of the largest stand of Ponderosa Pine in the world -- it stretches from near Kingman, Arizona to near Silver City, New Mexico.

Abert's Squirrels live only in Ponderosa Pine forests. If you are walking in the spring and see the tips of small branches laying on the ground (as in the upper picture on the right) you will know that the squirrels have been after some sweet treats. Just under the bark of the tree is the cambium layer. This is the layer where the sugar that the tree produces for nutrition by photosynthesis moves throughout the tree. Some trees are sweeter than others. The squirrels only nibble the branches off trees that supply the best treats.

Younger trees have dark bark and are sometimes called black-jacks. The older trees have a lighter bark and are called yellow bellies. If you are walking among the ponderosas on a warm day try scratching the bark of a yellow-belly on the sunny side with your fingernail and see if you can detect the odor of cinnamon or vanilla.

Pine cones are not the seeds of the trees; they are the seed carriers. Think of an ear of corn. The kernels are the seeds and the cob holds the seeds.

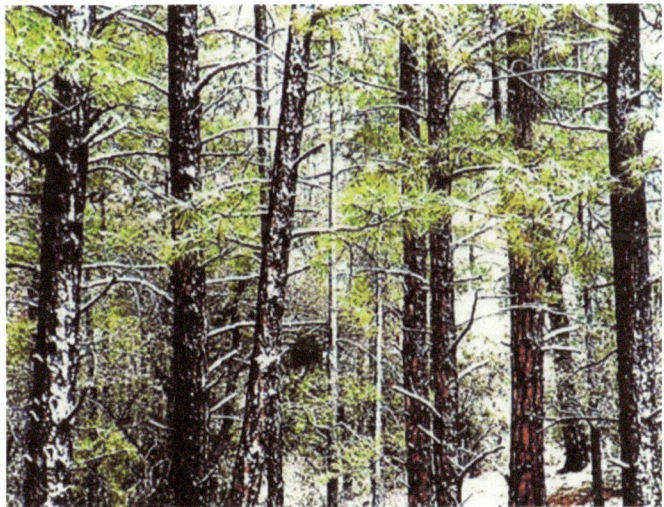

A Ponderosa Pine Tree That Was Struck By Lightning

On the evening of July 10, 2011 this ponderosa pine tree was struck by lightning. The tree appears to have been killed instantly because very little sap wept out of the gashes. You might wonder why it did not start a forest fire. Probably because the tree contained a lot of wet sap and people camped in the area said that the rain was coming down so hard that it sounded like a fire truck was pumping water on their trailers. They also reported that the lightning flashes and the thunder were occurring simultaneously -- proof that they were very close to the target of the lightning.

I have walked past this tree almost daily and have kept notes on its changes. For about the first year there was very little change. Most of the needles remained on the limbs and the cracks grew very little. I did not know whether it was dead or alive. In the spring of 2012 no new needles were produced so I concluded that it had died. By the spring of 2013 all of the needles had turned brown and almost all had fallen. By the spring of 2014 the cracks had widened but were not getting deeper. Acorn woodpeckers also started carving out large holes in the trunk. In January 2015, the top 25 feet broke off during a windstorm.

If you would like to see this tree park at the North Shore Park near the Lynx Lake Store and Café. Go down to trail 311 and turn right. After you pass the boat rental dock cove continue on to the next cove. After reaching the furthest indentation start to look for ponderosas on the left (lake) side of the trail. This tree is so close to the trail that the smallest child in the group will be able to touch it while standing on the paved trail. The GPS coordinates are Lat 34.519°N and Lon 112.38777°W. (The average of several readings.)

Why Are The Dead Trees Left To Rot?

This question is frequently asked when I am leading nature walks. There are two answers. The first is that many living things depend on dead trees. The second is that nothing in nature is wasted -- everything is recycled.

One of the first things that you can see that moves into dead trees are insects. The cracks provide refuge from rain and snow. This attracts insect-eating birds (like Northern Flickers). Then come the birds such as Cooper's hawks that eat other birds. Acorn woodpeckers store their winter food in holes that they drill in the trees. The bottom picture on the next page shows acorns in ponderosa bark. Eventually they will enlarge some of the holes and use them for nests. When they move on to new nests, other birds that cannot drill holes but prefer to nest in them (like swallows) will move in. As the bark loosens, bats will be attracted and take advantage of the shadows to sleep during the day. Eventually all of the drilling, nesting, and effects of microscopic organisms take their toll and one windy day the tree will fall.

After the tree falls, new creatures will take advantage of it. Carpenter ants move in and burrow in the wood making little "sawdust" piles around the log. Chipmunks will use the log for nesting. Skunks, raccoons and birds will tear the log apart looking for insects. After many years the log will disappear but it will still be providing food for many things as nature's recycling center works day-and-night, year-after-year.

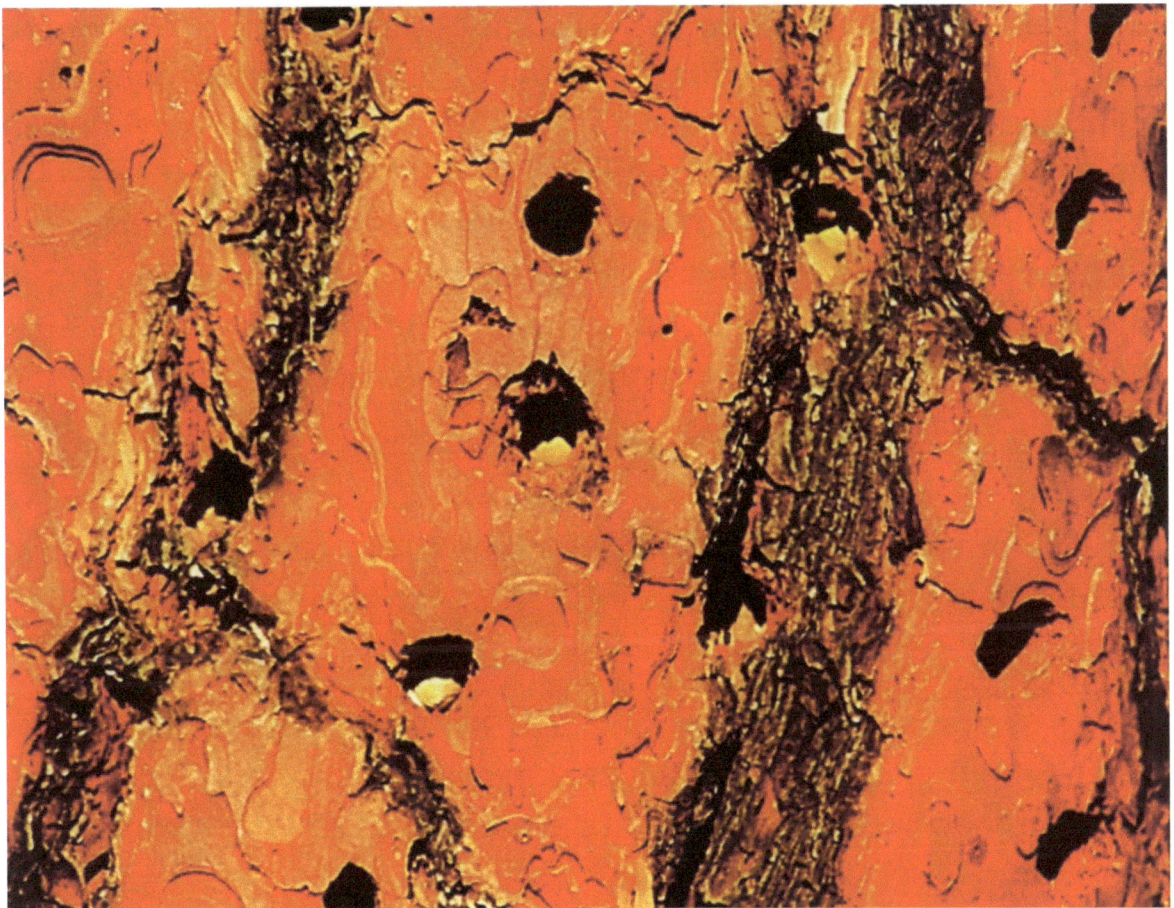

The Historic Role of Fire in Ponderosa Pine Forests

Dr. Sylvester Allred, who studied ponderosa pine forests for many years at Northern Arizona University, found that it takes about 27 months for a ponderosa pine needle to decompose after it falls off a tree. Ponderosa pines typically shed about 30% of their needles every year. After the thousands of years that ponderosa pines have been around we would probably have mounds of decaying needles hundreds of feet high if something did not clean the forest floor. That something is fire.

The earliest written records of the area state that people had little difficulty driving a horse and wagon through the forest – the trees were widely spaced. Historic fires probably only burned less than ten feet high and occurred about every five to ten years. This cleared out the dead needles, young ponderosas and competing plants that started to grow in the forest. Beginning in the 1940s the Forest Service began to fight every forest fire with the maximum effort to put it out. Also, many environmentalists felt that it was wrong to kill small plants so that big trees could grow. The huge crown fires that we see every summer now testify that the policies of the past seventy years have not been in the best interest of forest health.

The pictures on the opposite page were taken during a Forest Service prescribed burn in September 2011. Prescribed burns are the best attempt at restoring forests to their historic healthy state.

Fire scars on Ponderosa Pine and tree ring dating, as well as other techniques indicate that this area has not had a fire since the European settlers entered the area about 150 years ago.

Recovery after a Fire in a Ponderosa Pine Forest

After the prescribed burn in September 2011, I went to the site every month for one year and photographed the recovery. The most surprising thing to me was that there was new life after only one month. By the second month winter was arriving and there was little change for several months. By the spring of 2012, it was obvious that there was less underbrush and fewer pine needles on the ground, but as far as new growth was concerned it looked very much like the unburned land directly across Walker Road.

The first green plant that I noted on November 1, 2012 was the native grass Ring Muhlenbergia, commonly called Ring Muhly. This demonstrates how well a native plant has adapted to fire. Its roots were unharmed by a short period of fire.

The second plant was an indicator of something else. Mullein is an introduced plant in the United States. It seems to have been brought to Virginia by early colonists. Each plant produces up to 100,000 seeds when it blooms in its second year of life. The seeds are able to germinate after lying dormant for up to 100 years. It only grows in direct sunlight. It cannot compete with already established grasses. So when a fire removes its competitors it is nearly perfectly suited to spring to life.

Some small ponderosa pines were killed by the fire. This assists in restoring the forest to the times when a horse and wagon could easily be driven through the woodland. The thick bark of the larger trees protected them from the effects on a low-burning, short-term exposure to fire.

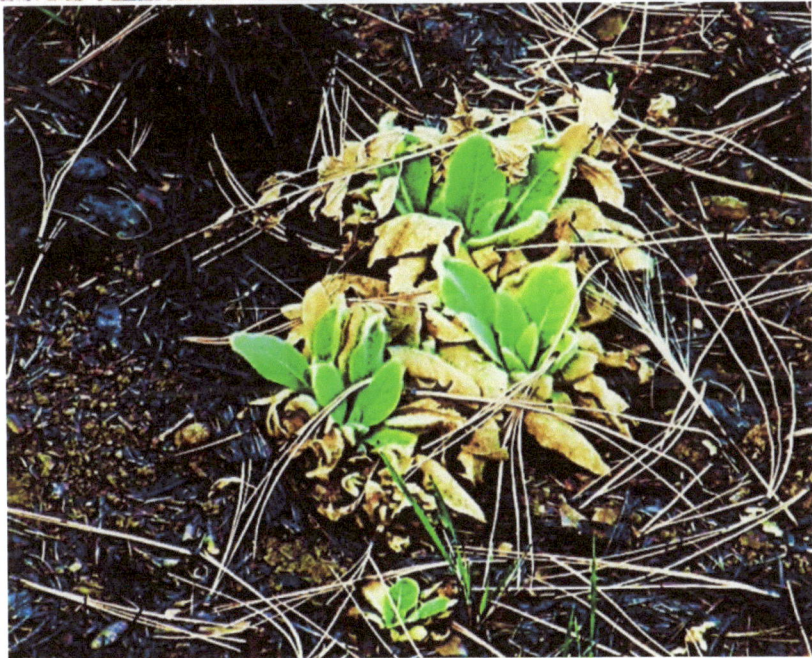

Alligator Juniper

The second-largest trees in the Lynx Lake area are the alligator junipers. These trees are easily identified by their bark that resembles alligator hide. Almost any child able to walk a trail will be able to answer the question, "What swamp critter's hide does this tree remind you of"? This thick bark provides the tree with excellent protection from the low-level, rapidly-moving fires that played an important role in forest health.

The habitat occupied by the alligator juniper is often referred to as oak-pinion-juniper woodland. In this area that is usually on the drier, south-facing hillsides. An interesting fact about these trees is that they do not produce annual growth rings. Instead they grow whenever they have a season with sufficient moisture. They might go for years without growing and then have two growth periods in one year. They may also be up to 1,000 years old.

What we call juniper berries are actually cones. They take two years to mature. The first year they are purple and the second year they turn brown as they ripen and fall off the tree. The berries grow only on the female trees.

The male trees produce only pollen which may turn the ground under them yellow in the spring. Alligator juniper pollen is a major source of allergy symptoms in the area when the male trees are in action.

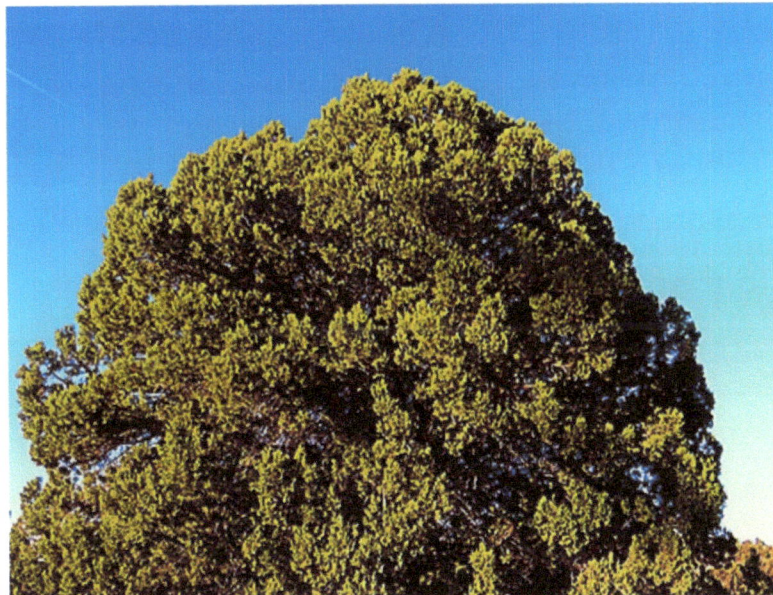

Arizona White Oak

I consider this to be the most interesting tree in the area. It grows in such a gnarly fashion that you can let your imagination run wild. One interesting activity to do with children is to have them look for "faces" in these trees. Finding these makes it easy to see why some ancient cultures believed that spirits inhabited oak trees.

The bark sometimes looks like an alligator juniper but it does not have the strong horizontal lines that the juniper has. It only takes one quick look to determine that the oak has leaves while the juniper has needles.

Many of these trees appear to have originated from misplaced acorns that were cached in ponderosa pines. Another fun activity for children is to look for "friendly trees" where Arizona white oaks and ponderosa pines are rubbing against each other. Sometimes you will even see an oak branch wrapped around a pine.

The bark of mature trees is quite thick and fire resistant as is the bark of Ponderosa Pine and Alligator Juniper.

The large lump in the lower left picture is a gall that formed in response to a mistletoe infestation. It is commonly called a burl.

There are four species of oaks growing in this area. If you are in the woods from mid- to late summer an interesting activity is to compare the differences in the acorns. The bark and leaves also assist in determining which is which. If you have difficulty in identifying a tree, remember that they hybridize.

Emory Oak

The Emory Oak is another abundant species, particularly on the drier, south-facing slopes. Its size lies between the Arizona white oak and the scrub oak. The quick way to see the difference is that the Emory oak is much less gnarly than the Arizona white and it has fewer small trunks than the scrub oak.

The oaks in this area are called live oaks because they keep their leaves over the winter. This gives the impression that they are alive as opposed to trees that lose their leaves in autumn and appear dead. Feel the tough, leathery leaves of this, and other oaks. This is an adaptation that allows them to lose less water into the air during long dry periods such as are common in May and June.

Scrub Oak

The name Scrub Oak is confusing. There are at least fourteen different trees and shrubs called scrub oak. What is called scrub oak in California is different from the scrub oaks that we have here and it is much different from what is called by that name in Colorado. This is why plants are referred to by their scientific names when specificity is necessary.

Scrub Oaks have many trunks growing closely together. They provide cover for many small mammals such as chipmunks and the many small bird species in the area. You can often discover that you are standing incredibly close to birds or small mammals concealed in these trees. They are secure because they are hard to see and can travel quickly through the thicket. Since they are seldom bothered in this habitat they tend to ignore people passing by.

The acorns produced by scrub oak provide valuable nutrition for mule deer, javelina and many other forest species.

Gambel Oak

This is an example of why the name Scrub Oak is confusing. In Colorado this is what is called "scrub oak". This is the only one of the four oak species in the area that has a leaf that would be recognizable as an oak leaf to people familiar with eastern forests. It is much smaller than the "mighty oak" of the eastern forests.

In this area they only grow where there is a good source of water such as around Lynx Lake and the riparian area along Lynx Creek. Deer browse their leaves but there are not enough of these trees here to be a major food source.

The acorns of the Gambel Oak are the first in the area to ripen and turn brown. Native American people used the acorns as a source of nutrition over the winter months. However, just as there are not enough trees to sustain the deer population, neither are there enough to sustain people.

Oak Galls

Oak galls are like something from a science fiction story. They are part of an oak tree that has been taken over and is usually controlled by an insect. The insect (commonly in the larva stage) uses the gall as protection from predators while it feeds off of the plant. Is that spooky, or what? The gall forms in response to chemicals injected by either the egg-laying female or the larva. Part of the gall may be due to the physical damage to the tree by the eggs being laid. As you can see in the pictures on the opposite page they take many forms. It seems like you can find some sort of gall on almost every oak.

An interesting activity for older children walking along the trails is to look for oak galls. First they learn to distinguish oaks from other trees and then they have the fun of discovering something new almost each time they find an oak.

SHRUBS, GRASSES, FUNGI AND LICHENS

Manzanita

The word "manzanita" means little apple in Spanish. However, the scientific name *Arctostaphylos* loosely translates to "bear food". However, humans also enjoy eating jelly made from the little apples that form in the late summer to fall.

The woody stems can be very attractive. The bark tends to peel off naturally and curls like wood shavings. When parts of the stem die and turn gray, new red growth may take place alongside the dead parts.

In this area they tend to bloom in mid-March and if there is sufficient moisture and it is not too cold they may bloom for six weeks. The little green apples form in late spring- to late-summer. The apples that do not get eaten by the end of summer will turn brown.

An unusual fact about Manzanita is that it does not have the very fine root hairs that most plants do. Instead they use microscopic fungi to absorb nutrients. This makes them very hard to transplant. If you dig up a wild plant not only will you be disturbing the forest, but breaking the law and will likely end up with a dead plant. If you want a Manzanita in your yard purchase one from a native plant store. It will have enough micro-fungi cultured in the soil to allow it to thrive.

Preparations made from the leaves have been used in treating urinary infections.

Sideoats Grama

This grass grows 2 to 3 feet tall. The tall stalks are called spikes. When it starts to "go to seed" you can sometimes see a pink to purple color in the spikes. The "oats" that hang from only one side of the spike are called spikelets. During the winter they have a reddish color.

Blue Grama

This is a short grama grass rarely getting more than 2 feet tall. Its spikelets grow on only one side of the spike (similar to side oats grama). However, these are more curved and are sometimes called eyelashes. It can be a fun exercise for younger children to examine the two different grama grasses and name them based on this difference.

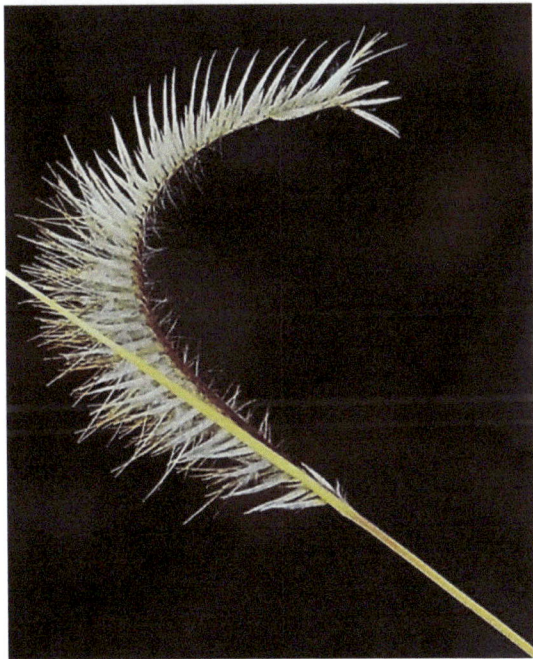

Mullein

Mullein was also discussed in the "Recovery after a Fire" section since it and ring muhly were the first plants that recovered in one month after the fire.

The plant on the left is wooly mullein and the one on the right is mock mullein.

There is a story that it was used by Native Americans in a manner similar to toilet paper but this is probably not very accurate. That is because it was introduced into the United States around 1640 in Virginia. It probably came west with the settlers of European ancestry so it has not had a chance to become widespread in the west until the last hundred years or so. It is used for this purpose by some people who are in the "back to nature" community.

There are several preparations that can be made from mullein to treat respiratory problems. They must be filtered to remove the tiny hairs because these can be very irritating to the throat.

Fungi Facts

Fungi include a vast number of organisms from microscopic in size to those that weigh tons. Modern genetic studies have shown that fungi are more closely related to animals than plants. They also have no chlorophyll (the stuff that makes plants green and produces energy) so, like animals, they require energy from outside sources.

What you see along the trails are the fruiting bodies of fungi. Many of these are commonly called mushrooms. One of the major roles that fungi play in our ecosystem is breaking down dead material so that nutrients can be recycled.

What you do not see along the trail is a symbiotic relationship between the roots of a plant and a fungus on those roots called mycorrhiza. In its recycling role the mycorrhiza supplies minerals dissolved in water to the plant. The fungus gets nutrition that it requires from the high-energy sugar produced in the plant leaves and transported to the roots.

Many cultures have used fungi as a source nutrition. However, if you are not well trained in fungal recognition then you are much better off picking your food off the grocery shelves than along the trail. Enjoy the observation of the many varieties of fungi along the trails but respect their ability to cause serious illness.

It is estimated that only 5% of the species of fungi have been formally classified. If you are a young person interested in a career in science then you might want to consider becoming a mycologist – a scientist who studies fungi.

More Fungi Facts

The Russula fruiting body (mushroom) pictured at the top of the next page is a very brittle mushroom.   Pushing its way up through the soil often causes a portion to break off. The fruiting body is the portion of the fungi life cycle involved with reproduction. The fruiting body will release spores. Spores are blown by the wind to a new location. If the conditions are right a new Russula organism will form. This will attach to the root of a plant and draw nutrition from it. In turn this mycorhizome will supply the plant with mineral-laden water that it has absorbed from the ground. Some species of Russula are edible but the ones with a bitter taste are more likely to cause vomiting or diarrhea.

The Amanita pictured at the bottom of the next page seems fairly easy to distinguish from the Russula because of the white spots. However, after several days the spots may wash off the amanita making identification more difficult.   Amanita is known for its hallucinogenic effects. Amanita are generally considered poisonous but there are few verifiable reports of death from people eating it. But, at the time that I was preparing this page *Arizona Highways* pulled its October 2013 issue off the market because an article in that issue failed to state that it was poisonous.

Both of these beauties are found in pine forests, so if you are on the trail after a few days of rain you may be able to spot some.

Earth Star

The earth star is unique among land-based fungi in its ability to move under its own power. When it rains it swells up and can raise itself an inch or so above the ground. The center of the top then bursts open and the spores fly out. There is a slightly greater chance of a breeze blowing just above the ground than there is flat on the ground. The spores are very tiny so they are easily blown around. They have a greater chance of landing in a good place to live than if they were not dispersed and all fell in one place. If you are on a trail in the early morning after a day or two of monsoon rains you may be lucky enough to spot a swollen one. I found this one on a rocky ledge about five feet above the road. I had just completed a walk and was not looking for anything else. As I was getting into my car I spotted it just at eye level. The bottom picture is what you are more likely to find. It is a dried up earth star that has already released its spores. I have no idea why but it seems that most of these are found under Manzanita. If you have extra water with you pour some on one of these and you will see it move. This has minimal impact on the environment since the spores have already been released.

Lichens

In this area lichens are found on rocks and trees. It is possible that some lichens on rocks are up to 10,000 years old.

Lichens are composite organisms. They consist of a fungus and an alga. It was thought that in these relationships both partners benefitted. However, examples have been found where one organism benefits and the other is unaffected, as well as one organism benefits and the other is harmed.

The algal portion can photosynthesize sugar from carbon dioxide and water using energy from the sun. The sugar then provides energy to both the algal and fungal portions of the organism. The fungal portion wraps itself around the algal portion preserving water so that it can be used to produce energy. The fungal portion also produces bulk to help capture more water and mineral-containing dust.

Some species of lichens are able to capture nitrogen from the air and fix it into stable compounds. As portions of the lichen break off and land on the soil the nitrogen is incorporated and is available to plants and microorganisms. Nitrogen is an essential nutrient for plants growing in soil.

It was thought that the two species could not live independently but that has now been proven wrong.

Some human cultures have used them as food but they are largely indigestible. Expect them to produce a large amount of gas.

A magnifying glass will provide fascinating viewing of lichens along the trail.

MAMMALS

Abert's Squirrel

Abert's squirrels live in ponderosa pine forests above 5,500 ft. Since the elevation of the Lynx Lake area is about 5,600 ft. they are well adapted to this area. They thrive in forests that have a mixture of tree sizes that you find in this area. They feed mainly on the seeds that are contained in the cones of the ponderosa. Trees that measure about 20 inches in diameter about 5 feet off the ground are the best seed producers, so look for Abert's squirrels in the fairly large trees.

Abert's squirrel nests can be hard to find because they are hardly ever less than 15 feet off the ground and are more likely to be up to 90 feet off the ground in very tall trees. The nests are built of chewed pine cones and twigs and are rarely more than 1 foot across. They are built in the crotches of branches, often on the southeastern side of the tree where they will be warmed early in the day by sunshine.

In the summertime they lose the tassels on their ears but grow them back again near the start of winter. Abert's squirrels are easiest to spot in February or March when they are very noisy and active during the mating season running up and down the tree trunks.

If you see a bunch of tips of ponderosa branches on the ground you are standing under a tree that the squirrels use to get sweet snacks. They will chew off the tip of the branch and then chew off another 2 inches or so of the small branch. Then they sit up and hold the short branch in their front paws gnawing off the outer bark similar to how people eat corn-on-the-cob. The inner bark (called the cambium layer) is where the tree moves the sugar that it has produced by photosynthesis and the squirrels like this sweet treat. Some trees are sweeter than others so some will not have their branch tips chewed off.

Cliff Chipmunk

This animal seems to exist only to convert seeds into food for those higher in the food chain. In some places they are abundant and in others you will hardly ever see them. They are easiest to spot when they are giving their high-pitched, shrill call – like a whistling sound.

It is unlikely that you will find a nest since they are usually underground or else high in trees. They are excellent climbers and will often sit very still warming themselves in the sun.

In the winter cliff chipmunks go into a deep sleep called topor. It is not as deep as true hibernation but close to it. When food is plentiful in the summer they do not gain fat the way many other mammals do; instead they fill the nesting area with seeds to eat when nothing else is available.

When you spot something that looks like a squirrel but is too small you probably are looking at a cliff chipmunk.

Rock Squirrel

These rodents are excellent earth movers. They dig tunnels that seem way too big for what they need. Sometimes the tunnels are located right next to trails. If you see a tunnel along a trail your first impulse is to think, "coyote". However, coyotes are much more secretive than this. You should be thinking, "rock squirrel". If you are some place that a rock squirrel does not want you to be you will find out that can make a lot of noise and keep it up until you decide to move.

Mule Deer

The best times to see deer are around sunrise and sunset. When you see them at other times of the day it is usually because someone is letting an unleashed dog run loose. In late winter when the does are pregnant and food is scarce they are hunkered down trying to conserve energy. Unleashed dogs chasing deer may just be the tipping point that causes the doe to have a miscarriage or die. In all of my time spent walking in the area I have only seen one buck with a full rack of antlers. It came running almost straight at me with a dog chasing right after it. I did not have time to take a picture before they were both past me.

Black-tailed Jackrabbit

The black-tailed jackrabbit is actually a hare, not a rabbit. The main difference between the two is that hares are born fully covered with fur, eyes open and within a few hours are able to run. Rabbits are born without fur, eyes closed and require the presence of their mother for at least several weeks.

Go back and look at the pictures of the mammals in this section. They all illustrate a little poem that will tell you if they are predator or prey:

Eyes in front
Loves to hunt
Eyes on side
Needs to hide

Where are the eyes on these animals? With the exception of the deer, they are all clearly on the sides. With eyes on the side animals are able to see above and behind their bodies. This is important when they could be attacked by something chasing them on the ground or swooping down from above. Predators need three-dimensional vision so that they can judge how far away the prey is when they are pursuing it, so their eyes point to the front.

Why are there no pictures of bears, mountain lions, bobcats, javelinas, raccoons or skunks?

Because bears, mountain lions and bobcats are top-notch predators that rarely show themselves during daylight. Raccoons and skunks are also active mainly after dark. This makes them hard to see and even harder to photograph. They are aware of your presence on the trail but choose to remain in hiding. Javelinas are occasionally seen in the area but not often enough that the casual walker will likely encounter them. This book is about what you are likely to see in the area.

REPTILES
AND
AMPHIBIANS

Arizona Mountain Kingsnake

One morning as I was leading a naturalist's walk at the Highlands Center for Natural History one of the participants spotted this pair of snakes mating. I always jump when I see these snakes because they resemble the desert-dwelling, poisonous coral snake. Some people memorize this poem to warn of danger:

> Red touch yellow
> Kill a fellow
> Black touch red
> Have no dread

One of the participants commented that he never thought he would be standing over two live snakes trying to remember the poem.

Arizona Black Rattlesnake

On another walk that I was leading a teenaged boy suddenly starting yelling, "That !@#$%^&* snake tried to bite me." Well it probably had not tried to bite him because if it had intended to, it would have done so. He had nearly stepped on an Arizona Black Rattlesnake. These snakes have a highly toxic venom but they do not like to waste it on things that they are not going to eat. Instead it gave him a very hard rap on the shin and crawled off to the side of the trail. Once it felt that it was a safe distance from us it coiled and showed its fangs once and then remained perfectly still. It stayed in that position while all of us who wanted to snapped pictures with our cellphone cameras. Mine didn't come out very sharp because I was still shaking too much. Later I went back to see if I could get a better picture. The snake remained there while I took several more pictures. However, since it was a dark subject lying in the shade with sunlight dappling the ground, the exposure was not very good but I was able to count five rattles. It was about 30 inches long. None of the seven of us heard any warning rattle even though we were only a few feet away from the boy.

Desert Striped Whipsnake

Look closely at this snake's tongue. Against the light-colored juniper twig you can see the tips of the forked tongue. This provides maximum surface area for tasting the air. Then notice the groove running most of the way back to the mouth. This concentrates the saliva and brings it rapidly back toward the brain. I was able to watch this snake for quite a while. If I remained motionless it would too. Finally I figured out that if I twitched, even slightly it would extend its tongue to examine the atmosphere. So I was able to get the camera ready, then move slightly and still be ready to take the picture. It worked!

These snakes are not poisonous but they will usually bite if you try to handle them.

Gopher Snake

This snake is not poisonous but it mimics a Diamondback Rattlesnake for defense. It will coil and shake its tail if it feels threatened. It often strikes with a closed mouth to scare predators away. It will hit people and dogs the same as it does true predators.

Our snake expert, Tony Krzysik, recommends that when you are planning a trip it is a good idea to become familiar with the snakes that you are likely to encounter and pay special attention to the appearance of those that are poisonous. Also remember that none of the snakes in this area are out to get humans or even pets. They only attack if they are threatened. They may see a dog trying to sniff them as a threat.

Schott's Tree Lizard

This lizard can change color to match its background. However, those living in this area are usually close to this color. Photographs do not always show colors as they look to our eyes, so do not place too much emphasis on exact color. There are other species of tree lizards, but this is the common, local species. The cross or chevron markings on the back are the identifying features of this lizard. It is almost always found on a tree, a rock or wall.

Insects, their larvae, and spiders compose most of the diet for these lizards.

Mountain (Hernandez's) Short-Horned Lizard

Sometimes called a horned toad but it is definitely a lizard. Notice how all the scales and bumps are slanted toward the back. All lizards are like this but here it is very noticeable. This makes it difficult for a predator to swallow them if they are caught from behind. It also breaks up their shadow making them harder to locate. Horned Lizards typically puff-up when threatened, making them not only seem larger to potential predators, but also more difficult for snakes to swallow. They are also capable of squirting blood out of their eyes to discourage predation from coyotes and raptors. In contrast to most other lizards these are rather slow moving. For safety they depend on their ability to match their skin color to their surroundings rather than speed. They tolerate cooler weather well so you may see these on days when there are no other lizards out.

A Tree Lizard That Has Re-grown a Tail

As a defense mechanism, many lizards have a tail that will break off when a predator grasps them. When this happens the trail thrashes about for a short time. If the predator goes after the tempting tail then the lizard may get away. It can grow another tail but things that are second-best never fully replace the original. Note that the replacement is not as highly colored as the rest of the body. It is also composed of cartilage rather than bone that was in the original tail.

What Do Lizards Eat?

This Plateau Fence Lizard scurried across the path in front of me. I got the camera up to my eye and made a careful approach. The lizard stuck its face down into the crack of a tree stump and came up with this grub. Evidently it was not the tasty feast that the lizard had hoped. It took one chomp and shook the grub out of its mouth.   The grub rolled off the stump and the lizard turned and walked in the opposite direction. They do eat grubs and insects – this lizard just did not want this particular grub. When termites are swarming, lizards will gather and swallow a termite every few seconds until the lizard's belly is bulging.

Other Interesting Facts about Lizards

The top left and bottom pictures are probably Plateau Striped Whiptails but it is impossible to tell them from Desert Grassland Whiptails without expert assistance. The other two are Plateau Fence Lizards.

The most common thing that you are likely to see on a casual walk in the area is a lizard. There are several species in the area and many individuals representing most species. Gila monsters generally do not live in this part of Arizona but there have been some found nearby.

Lizards cannot control their body temperature the way that mammals and birds can. Instead lizards have to bask in the sun to raise their temperature. This makes it fairly easy to study lizards that you see especially in the mornings before they get very warm.

Some lizards in the central Arizona highlands can inflict painful bites but none are harmful if they are not handled.

Notice the blue coloring on the underside of the Plateau Fence Lizard in the middle picture. If you watch one in the field for a few minutes you may see this lizard doing push-ups. This is a form of recognition and a display of dominance. It would be very dangerous for this lizard to have the blue coloring on its back because predators could easily spot it from above. So its distinctive coloration is barely visible until it decides to "show-off".

Most lizards like other vertebrates consist of both males and females in the population. However, approximately a third of Whiptail Lizard species are parthenogenic, (all females). The females lay eggs, producing young genetically identical to their mothers. The origin, advantages, disadvantages, and the ecological and evolutionary significance of Whiptail parthenogenesis is very complex and is still in active research.

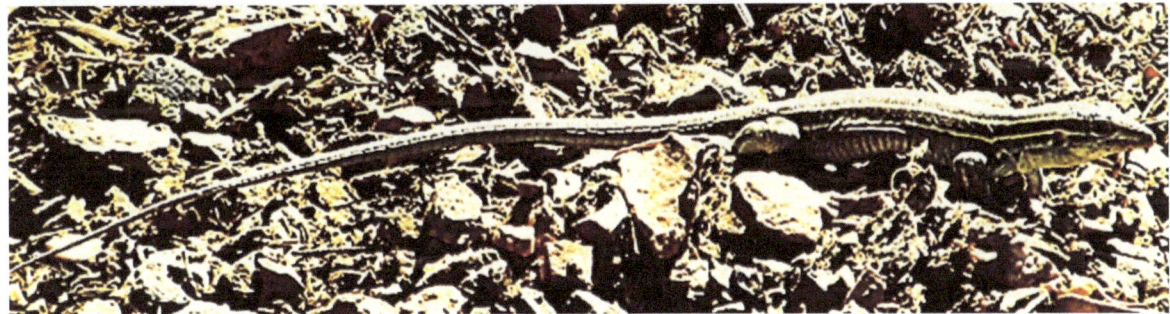

Canyon Treefrog

These are small frogs that grow to be only about 2 inches long. Despite their name they are not usually found in trees. They like to hide in cracks in rocks. By going very deep into cracks in large rocks they can survive winters, droughts and heat because of the protected from harsh temperature changes that this environment affords. They are able to change color to match their surroundings. The most common colors are green to brown with splotches. Canyon tree frogs are most active at night and eat insects and spiders. You will hardly ever find one that is not near a permanent source of water unless there has been a heavy rain, Canyon Treefrogs are excellent climbers.

American Bullfrog

This frog is rarely seen out of water. In fact it is pretty hard to see in the water because it will usually submerge as soon as it sees someone approaching. Look for them near the shore of Lynx Lake in the summer.

Bullfrogs are not native to Arizona. They are very competitive with native species. They will eat anything that they can get in their mouth. Since all of our native frogs and the young of lizards and snakes are smaller than bullfrogs they are all endangered by them. They also spread a fungus that is deadly to native species. Fortunately there are lots of great blue herons in this area that love to eat bullfrogs and keep them pretty well controlled.

Turtle Facts

Both of the turtles pictured on the opposite page as well as those in the picture opposite the section heading "Reptiles and Amphibians" are Red-eared Sliders. Young and female Red-eared sliders always have the characteristic red stripe on the side of the head but old males often do not show it. Like the American Bullfrog, these turtles are not native to the area.

Turtles evolved at least 12 million years before dinosaurs. However, they are in serious decline because of habitat loss, pollution, people eating them and being captured for sale in pet stores.

Turtles in this area are all aquatic. They live in (or very close to water). Turtles have fairly flat, streamlined shells. Since turtles prefer water it makes sense that they have webbed feet. They also tend to have long claws. As a group, turtles will eat almost anything. However, when it comes to individual species, many have quite narrow preferences.

When a female turtle is about to lay eggs she will dig a burrow. After the soft, leathery eggs are laid she will leave the area. When they hatch, the babies then dig their way out of the burrow and immediately live on their own. Turtles typically live to be about thirty to one hundred years old.

The top part of a turtle shell is called a carapace. The bottom section of the shell is called a plastron. The coverings of both the carapace and plastron are called as scutes. You can think of the scutes as being the turtle's skin while the shell is its skeleton.

It is legal to have one native turtle in your possession in Arizona but it is best to just enjoy looking at them and leave them alone. Releasing a native turtle is illegal.

INSECTS

AND

ARACHNIDS

Mormon Metalmark Butterfly

The caterpillar of this species feeds mainly on wild buckwheat which is a native of this area. The mature butterfly prefers to feed on yellow plants such as those seen along the area's trails and rabbit brush.

Common Buckeye Butterfly

This butterfly is found all the way from southern Canada to the northern parts of South America. They prefer areas with low-growing plants and some bare ground. Its colors can vary throughout the year so if the one you are looking at does not exactly match the picture it is probably the same species. They are able to get a drink of water from mud and damp sand.

Western Tiger Swallowtail Butterfly

Since this butterfly prefers to live near water you are most likely to see it on the shore of Lynx Lake or in the riparian (streamside) area of Lynx Creek. These large, showy butterflies are rarely seen sitting perfectly still. They can extract water from mud but will often drink directly from the lake or creek.

Arizona Sister Butterfly

In a rare stroke of luck I was able to capture a fairly sharp image of this butterfly in flight. It has been observed feeding on sap from an Emory Oak tree after a woodpecker had tapped into the trunk.

Monarch Butterfly

Monarch Butterflies are a species that is in a precarious situation partly because of the complicated life-cycle that it has. One life-cycle involves four different butterflies over the course of a year. Early in the cycle the butterflies hatch from their chrysalis and begin looking for a place to lay their eggs. When they find a mate the eggs are laid on a milkweed plant. After about four days baby caterpillars hatch. They then eat the milkweed. Only a milkweed will do for a Monarch, because the sap contains poisonous substances that the Monarch can tolerate but make it very distasteful for anything that tries to eat the caterpillar or butterfly.

After about two weeks of eating nothing but milkweeds the caterpillar will transform into a chrysalis. Over the next ten days, the caterpillar will undergo metamorphosis into the majestic Monarch. Over the next two to ten weeks, the Monarch will flit around feeding on flowers. The females will lay eggs that will become generation two for the year and then die.

The third generation will follow the steps exactly as the first and second generations did. The fourth generation will do exactly the same things as the first three generations with one major difference. The fourth generation butterfly does not die after a few weeks but migrates to Mexico, California and a few will winter over in Arizona. The fourth generation butterfly will live for six to eight months.

It is not very well understood how every fourth generation of Monarch Butterflies knows to migrate and how the first generation of the new year knows how to go back to the area where its ancestors lived three generations and a year ago.

Monarch Butterflies have white spots only on the black parts of their wings. The Viceroy Butterfly also has this same whit spot pattern but it also has a black stripe on its black wing. The Queen Butterfly and the Soldier Butterfly are easily confused with the Monarch.

Sphinx (Hawk) Moth

Since there are about 1,450 different species of these moths it is impossible for the average Highlands Center visitor to determine which is which. They are often mistaken for hummingbirds since they can fly very rapidly and can feed and drink while hovering. Its proboscis is more than twice as long as its body.

Wheel Bug

CAUTION: Wheel Bugs can inflict a painful bite if they are handled. The bite may take months to heal.

If you were to see the baby (larval) stage with its colorful red and black body on one walk and on the next walk spotted the adult stage, you would likely never guess that they are related.

The adult feeds on soft-bodied insects by injecting enzymes into their bodies to cause them to dissolve.

Wheel Bugs are sometimes mistaken for grasshoppers.

Damselfly

The preferred habitat for these insects is gently flowing streams and lakes – exactly what Lynx Creek and Lynx Lake provide. They can go underwater and remain there for 30 minutes or more. They feed on smaller insects and particularly those that live in water. They prefer to land on sunny places but seldom stay still for very long.

When a damselfly is resting its wings are held against its body.

Red (Orange) Skimmer Dragonfly

You can tell a dragonfly from a damselfly by the way it holds its wings when it is perched.   Dragonflies sit with their wings extended. Because their front and hind wings beat in opposite directions, they are some of the fastest flying insects and able to make almost instantaneous U-turns.

Dragonflies are almost always found around water. This is because the early stage of their life-cycle is spent underwater. One of their favorite foods is mosquitoes. They also eat bees, ants, flies and wasps.   Spiders, birds, frogs, and larger dragonflies will feed on them.

Grasshopper

Many insects are often confused with grasshoppers; these include bush crickets, katydids and locusts. One distinguishing characteristic is that grasshoppers usually have antennae that are shorter than their body. As you can see in the picture on the opposite page this is not always readily discernable. The right antenna appears to be about as long as the body, while the left one appears to have been broken off. Since this is not a textbook about exact identification let's call similar things grasshoppers.

Since they frequently land on bare spots they can be easily found by even young children. When startled they usually jump or fly over relatively short distance. This can be a source of amusement for young children. Notice that when they land they routinely turn to face a new direction. This habit makes it easier for them to escape should another getaway be quickly necessary.

Fly

Because of their habits of consuming fecal matter and decomposing organisms, flies are major vectors of infections. Over 100 diseases have been linked to fly transmission. Nonetheless, they are truly amazing in their own right. The female can lay as many as 9,000 eggs during her lifetime. This generally occurs after only one mating session. This occurs during the 14 to 28 day lifespan of an adult fly.

Note the large, red compound eyes. This type of eye gives the fly a great deal of resolving power. For the simple eye of a human to see as well as a fly it is estimated that each of our eyes would need to be about 30 feet across! Big trailers on the highway are 53 feet long, so one person would not be able to get into a trailer sideways.

Beetles

There are about 300,000 species of beetles in the world. Since many of them appear to be the same to a person walking along a trail, it is beyond the scope of this book to try to make an exact identification of them

Beetles have antennae, three pairs of legs and a tough shell called an exoskeleton. They do not have bones inside the shell. The characteristic that defines something as being a beetle is that their front pair of wings are called elytra. These front wings cover the body with an armor-like protection.

Some beetles are so small that they can hardly be seen without a magnifying glass. Others may be several inches long. Near the junction of Highway 69 and Interstate 17 is Big Bug Creek. It is fun to think about what the person who named that creek saw. However, this is not a game to be played with young children just before bedtime in an unfamiliar campsite.

Most beetles live solitary lives. This means that they live alone, with no family life. When they feel in danger, most beetles will hide or fly away. When you find one that stands its ground, it probably means that it produces irritating chemicals or that it will bite.

The head contains the mouthparts called mandibles. There is a compound eye on both sides of the head. The antennae serve as the nose and ears of the beetle.

The middle part of the body is called the thorax. Each of the three segments have a pair of legs. Each leg has five segments. Two of the thorax segments hold a pair of wings. The rear part is called the abdomen. This is where the digestive and reproductive organs are located. It breathes through spiracles in this area.

Ants

There are about 20,000 species of ants. They are very social insects. The number of ants in a colony can vary from dozens to millions. Since their survival depends on cooperation between specialized individuals they need to communicate. One way they can summon many individuals rapidly such as when food or an enemy is found is to tap their gaster (the large rear end) against the nest. Some have the ability to make squeaking or buzzing sounds to summon allies. They also produce pheromones – chemicals with distinct smells or tastes. They can distinguish friends from foes by detecting pheromones when they meet. The large ant mounds that are seen in this area are produced by harvester ants. Many can carry loads that are larger than their bodies for fifty feet or more without stopping to rest.

Water Strider

The best place to find water striders are along Lynx Creek on the Highlands Center property. At first glance these insects appear to have only four legs. That is because the poorly developed wings cover the short, front legs that have claws. Their mouthparts are developed for piercing and sucking. There are about 1,700 species of water striders. They are able to move over the water because their body weight is distributed so that they do not break through the surface of the water. They are covered with many, fine, water-shedding hairs that keep them from becoming water-logged. Should a wave submerge a water strider the bubbles around the tiny hairs allow it to rapidly pop back up to the surface.

Jumping Spider

There are about 5,000 species of jumping spiders. They all have four pairs of eyes with one pair centered just above the mouth. The placement of the eyes gives them a 360° view around their body. Once I saw a jumping spider on the opposite side of a window screen. I got my finger up very close. When I moved my finger it always followed it. They have two different ways of breathing so they can pursue prey relentlessly. When ready to strike they can make tremendous jumps of two to three times the length of their body.

Tarantula

THERE IS NO RELIABLE RECORD OF A HUMAN IN THIS AREA BEING KILLED BY A TARANTULA BITE. There is a possibility of a painful bite if you handle them. Please do not kill them and try to prevent others from doing so. One of their defense mechanisms is to brush off fine hairs that can cause itching and rash. These are unlikely to cause severe problems unless you inhale them or get them in your eyes. The tarantulas in this area live underground in burrows for most of the year. In the late summer the males come out of their burrows to seek the females who typically stay in their burrows. They eat insects and spiders. They generally reserve their venom for injecting into prey. If they do bite a human it is usually a "dry bite" into which little, if any venom is injected.

GEOLOGY

Phyllite

This is a metamorphic rock. It started out as volcanic ash but was changed into its present form by heat and pressure. After the volcanic ash was transformed, Prescott and Jerome were on separate pieces of land. These collided like a super slow-motion crash. The pressure from the crash caused the rock to form into the near-vertical parallel strips that we see today. There are quite a few outcroppings of phyllite in the area. One that I think is particularly interesting is on Trail 305 (Homestead) just north of where the trail crosses the road to the Lynx Lake North Shore parking area. In this area some of the strips are turned at right angles to adjacent strips.

Intrusive (Diabase) Dike

Magma is molten rock that forms the center of the earth. When it reaches the surface of the earth during a volcanic eruption it is called lava. Lava belongs to a group of rocks called igneous rocks – cooled from magma. Before the lava cools and hardens it flows much like hot wax from a candle. If it flows into a crack in an older rock it forms an intrusive dike. The dark material in the picture on the opposite page is a dike. Dark-colored lava is called basalt

Stretch Pebble

This rock formation most easily seen of the Highlands Center Trail #443 is one of the finest examples of this type of rock in the world. (Almost certainly the best example on a handicapped access trail.) The reddish pebbles are jasper, a type of chert formed from sediment most likely was deposited in an ocean. The gray pebbles are quartzite which was originally a sandstone. The other pebbles that are light colored were once volcanic tuff. To bring all three together it took the forces of an ocean, a volcano, and a tectonic plate collision. All of these point to the area's long geologic history – about 1.7 billion years.

Banded Iron

This amazing formation is most easily seen on Highlands Center Trail 442 just a short ways uphill from its junction with trail 305. . The gray layers are ancient forms of iron that can only form when there is no oxygen present. They settled to the bottom of the ocean. When photosynthesis began on the earth, oxygen was produced. This caused the iron to oxidize (rust). This formed the red layers. When all of the available oxygen was used, more gray layers were formed. The process repeated itself over many cycles. Today it is impossible for gray layers to form because there is always oxygen available.

SEASONS

Winter

It is easy to skip over winter but there are many things to enjoy if you dress warmly. The most obvious thing associated with winter is snow. You can observe different types of snow that are usually associated with the air temperature. Heavy, wet snows are occur when the temperatures around 30 degrees. Dry, powdery snows happen when the temperature is 20 degrees or colder. On a cold morning after a snow melt you can find leaves frozen in the resulting ice.

Birds to look for include bald eagles, hawks, mallards, cormorants, and ruddy ducks. They will be competing for limited sources of food and defending territories.

Spring

In this area spring is characterized by rapid changes between warm and cold. Think about how this limits things such as plant life. As warm weather begins to dominate notice there is an increase in plants such as manzanita, New Mexico locusts, willows, and cacti showing blooms. This in turn leads to an increase in insect activity. Butterflies are the showiest insects that become active now.

Bird activity greatly increases. Double-crested cormorants begin looking like they are having bad-hair days; great blue herons develop long, hairy-looking feathers on their head and necks as they search for mates. Birds begin their mating rituals such as feeding each other. This progresses to defending nests by driving away threatening species. Some birds will leave the area where they wintered and others will return from where they sought warmer weather.

Summer

The onset of summer usually coincides with the start of the monsoon rains. Massive thunderstorm and torrential rains are associated with clouds like the one on the opposite page. When you see this type of cloud it is time to be heading back to your shelter. When the rain stops look closely at water droplets on pine needles and other types of leaves. In the early morning after an overnight rain look for dew on grasses. After several days of rain many forms of fungi can be found.

Warm days are good times to spot reptiles. Snakes, bullfrogs and lizards (including horned lizards) are abundant in the area.

Warm evenings are great for sky watching. The Milky Way appears as a cloud of stars in the southeastern sky after about 9 PM when the sky becomes very dark. The Perseid Meteor Shower peaks each year around August 10th to 12th.

Autumn

On the lingering warm days you can often spot tarantulas on the move, but most insects will become less active. When the mornings are cold there may be interesting ice crystals on plants until the sun melts them.

Birds seeking refuge from colder climates such as waterfowl and dark-eyed juncos will be returning. In dry, brushy areas you may see quail running across the trail followed by many, tiny babies.

Trees such as aspens (near the Highlands Center buildings), Gambel oaks along Lynx Creek and the apple tree along trail 305 will show their peak colors. The opposite page shows a lemon verbena.

REFERENCES and FURTHER READING

Abbott, L. Geology Underfoot in Northern Arizona. ISBN 978-0-87842-528-0

Allred, S. Rascal the Tassel-Eared Squirrel. ISBN 978-0-938216-a88-9

Arizona Native Plant Society. Desert Grasses. No ISBN

Bailowitz, R. Seventy Common Butterflies of the Southwest. ISBN 978-187785-684-6

Bowers, J. One Hundred Wildflowers of the Southwest Woodlands. ISBN 0-911408-73-8

Magley, B. Arizona Wildflowers: A children's guide to the state's most common wildflowers. ISBN 1-56044-096-1

Moore, M. Medicinal Plants of the Mountain West. ISBN 978-0-89013-454-2

Neal, J. Geology at the Highlands Center for Natural History. No ISBN

Olson C. Fifty Common Insects of the Southwest. ISBN 1-58369-042-5

Sibley, DA. The Sibley Field Guide to Birds of Western North America. ISBN 0-679-45121-8

Smith, R. A Guide to Prescott and Central Highlands Trails. ISBN 978-0-9640308-0-2

Tekiela, S. Mammals of Arizona: Field Guide. ISBN 978-159193-075-4

Tomoff, CS. Birds of Prescott, Arizona. No ISBN

www.ingramcontent.com/pod-product-compliance
Lightning Source LLC
Chambersburg PA
CBHW060858270326
41935CB00003B/16